DO SOME THING!

Participant's Guide

Make Your Life Count

Miles McPherson

BakerBooks

a division of Baker Publishing Group
Grand Rapids, Michigan

Published by Baker Books
a division of Baker Publishing Group
P.O. Box 6287, Grand Rapids, MI 49516-6287
www.bakerbooks.com

Printed in the United States of America

Library of Congress Cataloging-in-Publication Data
McPherson, Miles.
    Do something! : participant's guide : make your life count / Miles McPherson.
       p.   cm.
    Includes bibliographical references.
    ISBN 978-0-8010-7249-9 (pbk.)
    1. Christian life—Textbooks. I. Title.
BV4511.M46 2009
248.4—dc22   2009035069

Unless otherwise indicated, Scripture is taken from the New King James Version. Copyright © 1982 by Thomas Nelson, Inc. Used by permission. All rights reserved.

Scripture marked NASB is taken from the New American Standard Bible®, Copyright © 1960, 1962, 1963, 1968, 1971, 1972, 1973, 1975, 1977, 1995 by The Lockman Foundation. Used by permission.

Scripture marked NIV is taken from the HOLY BIBLE, NEW INTERNATIONAL VERSION®. NIV®. Copyright © 1973, 1978, 1984 by International Bible Society. Used by permission of Zondervan. All rights reserved.

Published in association with Yates & Yates (www.yates2.com).

09 10 11 12 13 14 15   7 6 5 4 3 2 1

Contents

Dear Reader,

No one has done more good in and for this world than Jesus. During His three-year ministry, He established a moral standard for humankind that has yet to be improved upon. He healed diseases, cast demons out of the possessed, and raised the dead. But the most loving thing He did was to die for our sins, and undoubtedly the most powerful was to rise again.

But guess what He said about you?

YOU WERE CREATED TO DO SOMETHING GREAT!

> Most assuredly, I say to you, he who believes in Me, the works that I do he will do also; and greater works than these he will do, because I go to My Father.
>
> —John 14:12

Jesus did not say this because we could do something great, He said it because He needs us to do something great. We live in a world that desperately needs God's love. Just look at the brokenness that surrounds you. Anywhere you go, you're bound to see convalescent homes full of lonely, elderly grandmas and grandpas; jails overcrowded with lives ruined, some beyond repair; strip clubs full of "beautiful women," many whose self-worth is only skin deep. Abandoned kids, homeless families, battered women, overworked and medicated dads. Hospitals are full of the scared, the depressed, and the ill. People like you and me. I could go on and on—the list is endless.

DO Something! was not published to give you something to read but to inspire you to *do something* for one of these people for whom God's heart breaks. I challenge you to take this message seriously. Ask God to open your eyes to see what I am talking about, and more importantly, ask Him to turn your heart, like rivers of water, to inspire and anoint you to DO Something!

God bless,

Introduction to
DO Something!

Welcome to the *DO Something!* small group series—the vehicle that puts wheels on the book *DO Something! Make Your Life Count.* Get ready for what I hope will be a life-changing, *world*-changing experience. This introduction provides a brief overview before you attend your first group meeting.

Because the principles and stories in the book *DO Something! Make Your Life Count* are integral to this small group series, you will want to pick up a copy before the first meeting and read chapters 1–5, The Plan: An Overview of the 5 P's.

Session Format

Browse through Week 1 (pp. 13–26) to get an overview of how the different parts of the meeting are laid out. The teaching portion follows a fill-in-the-blank format. The circle format helps participants see how God's perspective intersects with our brokenness so that He can first do something *in* us and then do something *through* us.

Getting the Most Out of Your Experience

We all live busy, complex lives that tend to crowd out meaningful relationships. Deep friendships can't be formed with limited contact. One of the best ways to get the most out of this experience is simply to hang out with members of your group outside of group time.

Below are some practical ways you can grow closer to the people in your group:

- Give your group members a call to see how their week is going, get to know them better, and/or pray with them.
- Invite someone over for dinner.
- Babysit for a couple so they can go out.
- Establish a prayer chain.
- Sit with a fellow small group member at church.
- Have a special time of prayer with someone in your group. Use the AWCIPA prayer model (see appendix B in the book). AWCIPA sample prayers are found at the end of this study guide.
- Have a "guys' night out" or a "girls' night out."

Preparing for the Meetings

You may wonder if you will need to do anything between the meetings. The answer is yes! After all, this is a *DO Something!* series. A typical group meeting lasts about 90 minutes, which leaves 6 days and 22 ½ hours each week outside the group meeting to do the following:

1. An assignment called *Do Something* Next Steps, which you'll learn more about later.
2. A five-chapter reading assignment in *DO Something! Make Your Life Count* that pertains to the next small group lesson. Each chapter is just the right size for a daily devotional reading, making it easy to go through the material in a week.
   - Read chapters 1–5 before your first meeting.
3. The *DO Something* section at the end of each chapter. Although you're participating in an in-depth study of the book's concepts during this series, consider doing these activities. If you feel pressed for time, come back to them at a later date—they will help reinforce the decisions and actions you've taken throughout this small group series.

Week 1: Options for a Six- or Seven-Week Study

Week 1 of the six-week study will be a longer meeting than the remaining weeks because it combines the Orientation with the Overview of the Plan.

For a seven-week study, Week 1 is divided into two weeks. Zero Week begins with the Orientation on page 13 and ends with a get-acquainted potluck or refreshments. The next session then picks up with the Overview on page 17, moving you into the *DO Something!* experience.

FAQs

What if I have to miss a meeting or two?

Plan ahead, be proactive, and do something to keep up with the group. Make sure you have read the chapters in the book that will be covered during the weeks you miss. Set up a time with another group member or an accountability partner to go through the small group questions before you return to the next meeting. Ask the leader if you can borrow and watch the DVD.

What if I have a DO Something! *idea that is not listed in the back of the book?*

This list is only a start. Just as there are countless needs in the world, countless ideas will be needed to meet those needs. God is bound to give you a creative way to help someone. When He does, *do something* to put it into action!

How do I get my friends to come to meetings?

You may have friends and neighbors who are unwilling to come to church but might accept an invitation to a home to participate in the *DO Something!* series. Most people are interested in doing something to better their community. Invitations and a sample script that you can use when inviting new people to your group are in appendix B of this guide.

Do you need to be a Christian to do something?

Our desire, and God's, is to impact men and women for eternity, whoever they are. God has a desire to do something in and through everyone, Christian or not.

People to invite:

- family—immediate or extended
- friends
- co-workers
- neighbors
- church contacts

Small Group Misconceptions

I do not need to prepare for the meetings.

Be sure to read the chapters in the *DO Something!* book (consider using the book as a devotional) and complete the *Do Something* Next Steps from the previous lesson. This way you'll be prepared for the content of each small group meeting.

When the six weeks are over, the relationships I make will end.

Be prepared to make lifelong friends and even start another small group series together.

The accountability partner is only for the series.

In the second week of the series, you'll be encouraged to find an accountability partner to be your companion as you go through the series. But your relationship doesn't have to stop there. Generally speaking, it's easier to walk with God when someone is holding you accountable to the commitments you make for yourself.

The purpose of this group is to disseminate information.

In addition to providing information, the *DO Something!* series is designed to challenge you to do something. Each week you will have an assignment that will challenge you to do something. Take some risks and have fun with it!

The leaders will do all of the work.

A great place to begin doing something is in your group! Take advantage of opportunities to serve by watching the kids, serving food, contacting group members during the week, setting up and cleaning up each week, and so on.

Week 1: The Plan
Orientation and Overview

The goal of Week 1 is for members of the group to get acquainted, to talk about the basics of the session format, and to move into the *DO Something!* experience.

For groups who choose to divide Week 1 into two weeks, the first week—Zero Week—includes the Orientation and ends with a potluck or meal (pp. 13–16), and Week 1 picks up with the Overview of the 5 P's (pp. 17–26).

 ***Orientation***   *Zero Week*

Getting to Know Your Group . . . . 10 minutes

- Take a few minutes to get to know each other.
- Share: What is the number one reason you have chosen to be a part of this Do Something journey?

Introduction to the *DO Something!* Experience . . . . 10 minutes

- Watch the welcome message from Miles McPherson.
- Review the letter from Miles on page 5.
- Review the MyTown, USA, map on page 206 in the book.

What Is the Ultimate Goal of the Group? . . . . 5 minutes

1. Become a Do Something believer who is actively engaged in doing something obedient to God as an individual.

2. Accept the *DO Something!* Challenge on pages 205–8 in the book and become part of the solution to one of your community's problems. Join or start a ministry designed to bring Christ's love to your broken world.

Format of Weekly Sessions................................... 10 minutes

After a review of the previous week's material, the core of the meeting covers eight steps, represented by circles in your guide. Following is a description of each step.

Teaching

Participants will watch a DVD teaching from Miles McPherson while completing these four steps:

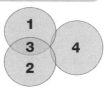

Step 1—God's Perspective

In Step 1 you will learn God's perspective on your life. God's perspective of your life is based on His unconditional love for you and His plans to use you to do great things in the world. The DVD teaching will guide everyone through the fill-in-the-blank questions about the lesson's topic. *An answer key is on page 78.*

Step 2—Our Brokenness

You will then skip down to Step 2 and look at your brokenness. Because of our brokenness, we have a very distorted view of our lives. We simply do not see ourselves like God does, and it's important for us to understand the extent to which our brokenness influences our decisions. The DVD teaching will guide everyone through the fill-in-the-blank questions about how our brokenness affects our perspective.

Step 3—Intersection

Step 3 lies in between the circles for Steps 1 and 2. Ministry happens when our brokenness intersects with and is submitted to God's ideal perspective for our lives. It is then that we must make a decision to do something to submit ourselves to His plan for our lives.

14

The DVD teaching will guide everyone through the fill-in-the-blank questions about the lesson's topic.

Step 4—Do Something

Once you experience what God wants to do *in* you, you are ready for Him to do something *through* you. In Step 4 you will learn about applying your internal "do something" to help someone else in his or her time of need. Ministry happens when you apply the changes that God has made in your life to help someone else.

Discussion

After viewing the DVD teaching, a group discussion follows the same four steps. This is your opportunity to internalize the lesson and discuss how it applies to you.

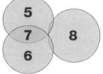

Step 5—God's Perspective

Discuss what you've learned about God's perspective on your life.

Step 6—Our Brokenness

Discuss how your brokenness can distract you from God's perspective on His plan in your life.

Step 7—Intersection • Next Steps Preview

Now that you have learned two opposing views—God's perspective and how you view life through your brokenness—it is time to discuss what you need to allow God to do in your life to bring about His desired change. Keep in mind: what God does *in you* is going to lead to His doing something *through you.* This step will help prepare you for Step 8 and the practical *Do Something* Next Steps that you will complete during the week.

Step 8—Do Something • Next Steps Preview

The last discussion will prepare you to practically apply what you have learned and experienced to help someone who is in need.

You will have three *Do Something* Next Steps options. Each step builds on the previous one, starting with something simple in the first step. *Do only what you feel comfortable doing.*

> **Crawl**—This will usually be something simple you can do alone and most often contains a form of planning.
>
> **Walk**—This step is a little more aggressive *do something* and usually involves contacting someone via email, phone, or letter.
>
> **Run**—This step will usually involve making personal contact with someone.

Each week you will be encouraged to bring back a report on what you did.

You'll also be asked to find an accountability partner to help you stay on track as you work through this study.

NOTE: "(*Optional*)" is placed next to questions you can respond to as time allows.

Do Something Next Steps

The *Do Something* Next Steps are what you are responsible to do on your own outside the group meeting. These pages are designed to guide you through what you have been challenged to do in Step 8 of the week's lesson. You can also use these pages as a journal to record what happens.

Small Group "I Do's"

Review the Small Group Guidelines in appendix A (pp. 101–2).

Prayer (Zero Week Only)

Break (Zero Week: Potluck • Week 1: Short Break)

Use this snack or meal time to complete the sign-up sheets for contact information, refreshments, and child care as your group leader requests.

 ## *An Overview of the 5 P's*

Preparation: Advance Work
Purpose: Obedience
Pain: It Doesn't Have to Only Hurt
Power: The Ability to Do
Passion: Never Give Up

God's plan for Jesus' life is the plan for *your* life too.

> Most assuredly, I say to you, he who believes in Me, the works that I do he will do also; and greater works than these he will do, because I go to My Father.
>
> —John 14:12

According to Jesus, you were created to do something great!

Prayer Time . . . . 10 minutes

Dear Lord, thank You for Your plan for our lives. We want to do something great. Jesus, we believe that You love us and will do great works through us. Please help us understand exactly what we need to do to fulfill our role in Your plan. In Jesus' name we pray, Amen.

Icebreaker . . . . 10 minutes

Think about a time when you had a part in making a plan come together successfully—whether with your friends and family (party, reunion, trip); with your church (event, service project); at work (project, meeting); or elsewhere. What did you find most fulfilling about this experience?

Bible Story: Thursday Night—*John 14:12*

17

Watch the DVD and fill in the blanks below.

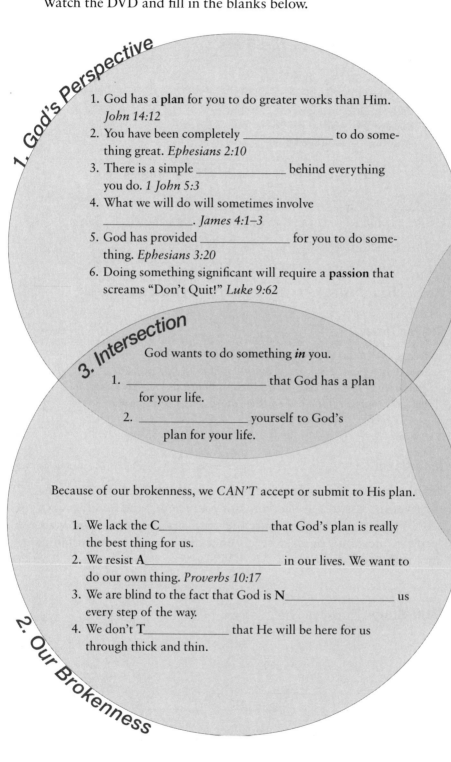

1. God's Perspective

1. God has a **plan** for you to do greater works than Him. *John 14:12*
2. You have been completely _____ to do something great. *Ephesians 2:10*
3. There is a simple _____ behind everything you do. *1 John 5:3*
4. What we will do will sometimes involve _____. *James 4:1–3*
5. God has provided _____ for you to do something. *Ephesians 3:20*
6. Doing something significant will require a **passion** that screams "Don't Quit!" *Luke 9:62*

3. Intersection

God wants to do something *in* you.

1. _____ that God has a plan for your life.
2. _____ yourself to God's plan for your life.

Because of our brokenness, we *CAN'T* accept or submit to His plan.

1. We lack the **C**_____ that God's plan is really the best thing for us.
2. We resist **A**_____ in our lives. We want to do our own thing. *Proverbs 10:17*
3. We are blind to the fact that God is **N**_____ us every step of the way.
4. We don't **T**_____ that He will be here for us through thick and thin.

2. Our Brokenness

4. Do Something

God wants to do something *through* you.

1. God's plan is designed to do something to you and then do something through you.
2. Whatever God does _____ you is always for the benefit of someone with a specific need.
3. Acknowledge that there are people _____ who will benefit from your fulfilling God's plan in your life.

Read John 14:12 together. Describe what you think it means to be able to do greater things than Christ.

5. God's Perspective

1. God has a plan to do something through your life on behalf of someone else. If you let go of all of the nervousness, doubt, fear, and excuses, what type of help do you think you would really enjoy providing for people?
2. Is there a specific group of people you feel God has planned for you to help? Why do you feel that?
3. Knowing that God has a plan for your life, how does that knowledge impact your decision-making process in your daily life? Give a specific example.

7. Intersection • Next Steps Preview

1. After hearing a brief overview of the five P's, which do you think is the hardest P for you to fully embrace? Why? Describe the obstacle that will be first to get in your way.
2. If you could lean on the help of one person to encourage you through this process, who would it be?

1. Describe a time you were a part of something that you believed in but that lacked leadership, organization, and vision. How did you react? How did this make you feel? How did it impact your participation?
2. In what ways have you had a similar attitude toward God and His plan?
3. (*Optional*) Is there a part of you that doubts that God has a plan? Why?

6. Our Brokenness

8. Do Something · Next Steps Preview

Remember, Jesus said that if you believe in Him, you would do greater things than He did (John 14:12).

As a group, review these Next Step options:

Crawl: Begin a journal describing the kind of person you think you could become if God were to refine His plan in your life. For example, what behaviors and attitudes would be different? What fears would you need to overcome? What new disciplines would you need to begin? Dream big!

Walk: Describe the type of person you would like to become and identify someone you want to help if God's plan was fulfilled in your life. What changes in behavior or perspective would result in that person as a result of you doing something for them?

Run: Identify and explore a community organization or ministry that provides the kind of help God has created you to provide. Gather information on how they do what they do and why. Join them!

LEADERS: *Turn to Wrapping Up Week 1 on page 100.*

Group Prayer . . . . .5 minutes

Dear Lord, we know that You have a plan to put us in a position to do something great through our lives. We ask that You reveal Your plan to us each day. Please give us the faith to allow You to lead us through that plan.

Notes

DO SOME THING Next Steps

God must do something in me before
He can do something through me.

Of all of the P's, the one that scares me the most is _____
because _____

The biggest internal obstacle I will need to overcome is _____
_____

Explain why it has been so hard to overcome. _____
_____
_____
_____

Accountability Partner

I will find an accountability partner by _____ (Date).

Suggested approach when asking someone to be an accountability partner:

"How are you? First, let me say I have great respect for you and your faith in God. I have a desire to grow in my relationship with God and I would like you to hold me accountable to meeting certain deadlines I will be setting for myself. As part of the weekly Bible study that I am a part of, I would like to ask that you be the person who signs off on my assignments. This will help me to be faithful to complete them and ensure that I put myself in the best position possible to grow spiritually."

My accountability partner is _____

God has a plan to do something
through me for someone.
Dream Big!

Crawl

If God were to refine His plan in my life . . .

- What behaviors, internal and external, would be different?

  _____

  _____

- What fears would I like to overcome?

  _____

  _____

- What new disciplines would I begin?

  _____

  _____

- How would this change the person I am?

  _____

  _____

Walk

Describe the type of help you would like to provide to someone by completing this sentence:

- I would like to help someone who is struggling with . . .

  _____

- After I help them, I would like them to be able to . . .

  _____

Run

Within the next _____ days, I am going to visit a _____ _____ (community organization or ministry).

- While at this organization/ministry, I learned that God wants to use me to _____

  _____

- Based on what I did this week, what did God show me about myself?

  _____

  _____

- What did God show me about Himself?

  _____

  _____

Week 1 completed _____ (Date)

Accountability partner's signature: _____

Prayer

Dear Lord, I know that You have a plan to put me in a position to do something great through my life. I ask that You reveal Your plan to me each day. Please give me the faith to allow You to lead me through that plan.

Preparation for Next Week

Read chapters 6–10: Preparation.

Make notes on your calendar for those items you have signed up to do at group.

Week 2: Preparation
Advance Work

God prepared *you* to do something
just as He prepared Jesus to do something.

> For we are His workmanship, created in Christ Jesus for good works, which God prepared beforehand that we should walk in them.
>
> —Ephesians 2:10

Before you were born, God made all of the necessary preparations for you to do something that will make your life count.

God prepared you with every necessary natural and spiritual skill, along with the ideal opportunities in life to use those skills to help people. He has also prepared you with all of the encouragement you will ever need to get you through the difficult times. You are more prepared than you know.

Prayer Time . . . . 5 minutes

Dear Lord, thank You for preparing us to do something. Please reveal to not only our minds but our hearts all the preparations You have made. Give us the faith to trust in those preparations. Thank You, God. In Jesus' name we pray, Amen.

Next Steps Review . . . . 10 minutes

Icebreaker . . . . 10 minutes

Do you tend to be a person who prepares too little or too much? Briefly share an example. What are the dangers of being underprepared or overprepared? How does one strike the balance?

. . . .

Bible Story: Satan Tempts Jesus—*Matthew 4:1–11*

Watch the DVD and fill in the blanks below.

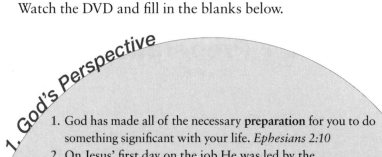

1. God's Perspective

1. God has made all of the necessary **preparation** for you to do something significant with your life. *Ephesians 2:10*
2. On Jesus' first day on the job He was led by the _____ _____ into the wilderness. *Matthew 4:1*
3. God prepared the _____ for Jesus and us to use. *Matthew 4:1–11*
4. God prepared us with _____ as a means of communicating with Him. *Luke 5:16*
5. God created and prepared _____ as a means of having a relationship with Him. *Romans 12:3; Hebrews 11:6*
6. God prepared the circumstances and _____ for us to do something. *Galatians 4:4*

3. Intersection

God wants to do something *in* you.

1. Give God the first opportunity to help you.
2. Instead of trusting in myself, I will place my faith in the _____ that God has made for me.

1. The preparations God has made for us can only be accessed by _____. *Hebrews 11:1, 6; 2 Corinthians 5:7*
2. When we walk by sight, faith plays _____ like a soldier in a war movie.
3. We do not trust in God's preparations because we think we have _____ ideas than God. *Proverbs 14:12*

2. Our Brokenness

4. Do Something

God wants to do something *through* you.

1. God has prepared a

   _____ with
   a need for you to do something
   to help.

2. God has prepared the

   _____

   for you to help someone.

Read Ephesians 2:10.

5. God's Perspective

1. What's one advantage we have in serving God in this culture as compared to the culture of our parents?
2. (*Optional*) How can you leverage those advantages?
3. In addition to the tools of faith, the Bible, the Holy Spirit, divine appointments, and prayer, what are some other ways God has prepared you to do something? Answer by completing this sentence:

   God has prepared me to do something by giving me:

   a. _____
   b. _____
   c. _____

7. Intersection • Next Steps Preview

Based on the list of tools (or weapons) with which God has prepared you to do something, identify one tool you think you need to improve your dependence on the most. Develop a plan to implement this week that will help ensure that you depend on it more.

1. Read Zechariah 4:6. Describe an incident when you relied on your own preparations and it did not work. Examples: Working hard instead of praying hard. Man's wisdom instead of God's Word. Trusting in what you know instead of trusting God by faith.
2. (*Optional*) Discuss the types of excuses or obstacles that get in the way of you relying on God's preparations.
3. Which of the tools mentioned or identified by your group do you think you need to improve on most? Why? What problems do you encounter if you neglect using this tool?
4. (*Optional*) Read Galatians 5:16–17. Can you give one example of when your faith was trying to get you to trust in God's preparation and you shot it dead by ignoring what it was telling you?

6. Our Brokenness

8. Do Something • Next Steps Preview

Identify one person who you think will benefit from your learning to depend on God's preparations—for example, someone for whom you can pray or share a Scripture with or serve by faith. Maybe God has just brought someone into your life under unexplainable circumstances. Maybe it's an old acquaintance you haven't seen in a long time. Maybe it's a neighbor or a co-worker or a family member who is struggling.

As a group, review these Next Step options:

Crawl: Identify, write down, and commit to memory the five tools with which God has prepared you to do something.

Walk: Describe to someone you trust a person and situation you believe God has specifically prepared you to help.

Run: Take one practical step to reach out to that particular person with your faith, the Bible, prayer, or something God has given you. Discuss ideas with your group on how to best do something.

Bring back a report on what happened.

Group Prayer . . . . 5 minutes

Dear Lord, thank You for preparing us for everything You would ever ask us to do. We are more confident than ever before that there is no reason for us to be fearful or hesitant to step out by faith. We look forward to learning how to take full advantage of the preparations You have made for us.

Notes

 **Next Steps**

God must do something in me before
He can do something through me.

These are the five tools God has prepared us with:

- ### *The Holy Spirit—the Invisible Man*

Acknowledge the Holy Spirit each day by speaking to Him as though He was standing next to you. Ask Him to

- guide you into truth (John 16:13),
- remind you of what Jesus said (John 14:26),
- convict you of your sin (John 16:8), or
- help you pray (Romans 8:26).

- ### *Faith*

Whenever you make a major decision, by faith ask the Invisible Man—the Holy Spirit—to guide you into truth. Trust what you feel He is telling you to do. Keep in mind it will always be in line with God's Word.

- ### *God's Word*

Memorize Hebrews 4:12.

- ### *Prayer*

To get you started, use the AWCIPA prayer model (p. 209 in the book) and samples (p. 107 in this guide), and each day this week spend two minutes on each letter, praying for more of God's power in your life—a total of twelve minutes a day. Feel free to insert your own verses and, of course, your own prayers. Bring a Bible, pen, and paper.

Set your time and place for each day:

	Sun	Mon	Tue	Wed	Thu	Fri	Sat
Time							
Place							

- ### *Divine Circumstances*

Identify one circumstance that you can see as designed by God for a specific purpose. Describe this situation and what you think God wants you to do in it in order to glorify Him:

> I believe that God has placed me in [describe the situation] so that I can help [describe the person and how God wants you to help them].

Dependence Plan

Based on the tools with which God has prepared you to do something, identify one that you think you need to depend on more. Develop a plan to implement this week that will help you toward that.

For the next five days, I am going to actively (check one)

__ rely on the Holy Spirit
__ exercise faith
__ live out God's Word
__ practice prayer
__ recognize divine circumstances

> *God has completely prepared me*
> *to do something for someone.*

Identify one person whom you think will benefit from your learning to depend on God's preparations. For example, someone for whom you can pray or share a Scripture with or serve by faith. Maybe God has just brought someone into your life under unexplainable circumstances. Maybe it's an old acquaintance you haven't seen in a long time. Maybe it's a neighbor or a co-worker or a family member who is struggling.

Crawl

Commit to memory five ways God has prepared you to do something by writing out this list of tools five times each:

Holy Spirit   Faith   Word   Prayer   Circumstances

35

Walk

Describe to someone you trust—like your accountability partner—a specific relationship that you believe God has set up, through His preparations, for you to help.

- God has set up a special relationship with _____

- I believe it is a "God thing" because _____

  _____

- I will describe this to _____ by _____ (Date)

Run

Take one step to reach out to bless that person with your faith, the Bible, prayer, or something God has given you. With a trusted friend, like your accountability partner, discuss ideas on how to do this.

- I am going to bless _____ (Name) by _____ (Date)

- What are you going to do? _____

  _____

Week 2 completed _____ (Date)

Accountability partner's signature: _____

Prayer

Dear Lord, thank You for making all of the necessary preparations for me to do something. I want to become completely dependent on them. Please renew my mind and convert my heart that I will trust in the preparations You have made. Thank You for being patient with me.

Preparation for Next Week

Read chapters 11–15: Purpose.

Make notes on your calendar for those items you have signed up to do at group.

Week 3: Purpose
Obedience

Jesus' purpose in life is *your* purpose in life.

> Jesus answered and said to him, "If anyone loves Me, he will keep My word; and My Father will love him, and We will come to him and make Our home with him."
>
> —John 14:23

God's purpose for your life is to love Him by simply doing something obediently.

Your life will only count for something eternal if what you *do* is motivated by loving God. Loving God has nothing to do with emotion or feeling; it has everything to do with faith-based *obedience*. The only true measure of your love for God is your level of obedience to Him.

Prayer Time . . . . 5 minutes

Dear Lord, we each want to fulfill our life's purpose by loving You. We thank You that You have prepared us to love You. Please increase our desire to love You, God. In Jesus' name, Amen.

Next Steps Review . . . . 10 minutes

Icebreaker . . . . 10 minutes

What are the benefits of knowing and understanding one's purpose in life? How does one discover the purpose of life?

Bible Story: The Greatest Commandment—*Matthew 22:37–40*

Watch the DVD and fill in the blanks below.

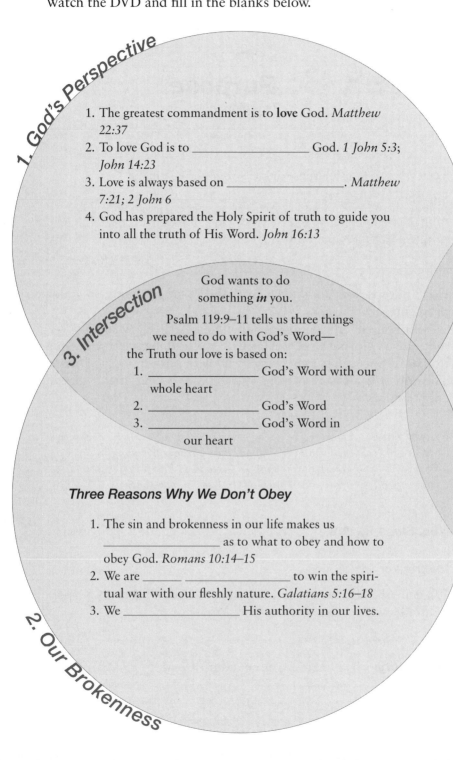

1. God's Perspective

1. The greatest commandment is to **love** God. *Matthew 22:37*
2. To love God is to _____ God. *1 John 5:3; John 14:23*
3. Love is always based on _____. *Matthew 7:21; 2 John 6*
4. God has prepared the Holy Spirit of truth to guide you into all the truth of His Word. *John 16:13*

3. Intersection

God wants to do something *in* you.

Psalm 119:9–11 tells us three things we need to do with God's Word—the Truth our love is based on:

1. _____ God's Word with our whole heart
2. _____ God's Word
3. _____ God's Word in our heart

Three Reasons Why We Don't Obey

1. The sin and brokenness in our life makes us _____ as to what to obey and how to obey God. *Romans 10:14–15*
2. We are _____ _____ to win the spiritual war with our fleshly nature. *Galatians 5:16–18*
3. We _____ His authority in our lives.

2. Our Brokenness

4. Do Something

God wants to do something *through* you.

1. If I love God, I must _____ Him.
2. If I love others, I must help them _____ God.
3. My purpose is to ensure that all of my relationships are obedient to God.

Read 1 John 5:3 and Matthew 25:21.

5. God's Perspective

The biggest blessings come when we are obedient to God's Word.

1. Identify a time when your life (or part of your life) was completely in line with God's Word. What benefits did you experience because of that?
2. Describe someone you know whose life is in line with the Bible. What benefits do they experience?

7. Intersection • Next Steps Preview

With the help of a friend, complete the following sentence and find a Scripture verse that addresses the need:

Based on my friend's input, the part of my life that most desperately needs to get in line with God's Word is _____
_____.

My first step to accomplish that is to memorize
_____.

Often disobedience looks good! It promises to bless us but only disappoints.

1. Describe a time when you made a decision based on your emotions instead of God's Word. What was the result? (Note: Emotions can be helpful but can also be misleading at times.)
2. Describe a time when you made a decision based on peer pressure or fear of man and, as a result, were misled. What was the result?
3. (*Optional*) On a scale of 1–10, how much do you depend on
   Your emotions? _____
   Peer pressure? _____

6. Our Brokenness

8. Do Something • Next Steps Preview

Many of us have relationships that are not in line with God's Word. They may be sexually inappropriate, dishonest in a business practice, or filled with gossip. One of the best ways to do something for a friend is to align *your* relationship with God's Word.

As a group, review these Next Step options:

Crawl: Identify a person in your life with whom you have a strained or unwholesome relationship and describe in your journal the behavior you believe you need to address and confront.

Walk: Write and send a letter to that person, apologizing for your role in the relationship and expressing your desire to correct the situation.

Run: Set up a meeting with that person and develop a plan together to bring your relationship in line with God's truth.

Bring back a report on what happened.

Group Prayer . . . . 5 minutes

Dear Lord, thank You for giving us such a simple and clear purpose of obeying You. We want to be known by You as someone who will do what You say when You say it and in a way that pleases You.

Notes

 **Next Steps**

*God must do something in me before
He can do something through me.*

Fill in your answer from Step 7 for this sentence:

Based on the discussion with my friend, the part of my life that most desperately needs to get in line with God's Word is . . .

_____

Explain why it needs changing and what that change could look like.

_____

_____

The Scripture verse from Step 7 is _____. To help you memorize it, write out the verse 7 times and say it out loud each time.

1. _____

_____

2. _____

_____

3. _____

_____

4. _____

_____

5. _____

_____

6. _____

_____

7. _____

_____

*God has established a clear purpose to
do something through me for someone.*

Crawl

After identifying a relationship in your life that is strained or unwholesome, describe in writing the behavior or attitude that needs correcting, and then pull out your Bible and search for verses that apply to each one.

I have a friend named _____ and the parts of our relationship that dishonor God are

1. _____

This is not in line with God's Word that says . . .

_____

2. _____

This is not in line with God's Word that says . . .

_____

3. _____

This is not in line with God's Word that says . . .

_____

4. _____

This is not in line with God's Word that says . . .

_____

Walk

Write and send a letter to that person, apologizing for your role in the relationship and expressing your desire to correct the situation.

Dear _____,

I want to apologize for allowing our relationship to dishonor God by . . .

Please forgive me for not bringing God's standard to light.

Your friend,

Add a prayer to your note or letter.

> Dear Lord, I have a desire to bring my relationship with _____
> in line with Your Word. Please give us the courage and faith to trust
> that obeying Your Word will actually enhance our relationship and
> our ability to honor You with our lives.
>
> Thank You for Your patience with us.
>
> In Jesus' name, Amen.

Run

Set up a meeting with that person and develop a plan together to
bring your relationship in line with God's truth.

Meeting date _____ and time _____

Place _____

Begin the email, phone call, etc., with something along these lines:

> Hello, _____, I would like to get together and talk
> to you about how we can improve our relationship and secure God's
> blessing on it.

And at the meeting, introduce the purpose in this manner:

> If I really love you, I need to help you obey God or in the least not
> distract you from obeying God. By allowing _____ in our relation-
> ship, I have not done that and I am sorry . . .

Describe the unacceptable old, disobedient behavior and the desired
obedient behavior.

Old Behavior

_____

New Behavior

_____

Week 3 completed _____ (Date)

Accountability partner's signature: _____

Prayer

Dear Lord, I want to fulfill Your purpose in my life, not my purpose. Please reveal to me the areas in my life and relationships that are not aligned with Your Word. Please give me a desire to hide Your Word in my heart and obey it.

Preparation for Next Week

Read chapters 16–20: Pain.

Make notes on your calendar for those items you have signed up to do at group.

Week 4: Pain
It Doesn't Have to Only Hurt

Jesus turned pain into something positive
and He can do the same for you.

> Where do wars and fights come from among you? Do they not come
> from your desires for pleasure that war in your members?
>
> —James 4:1

If you don't want pain merely to hurt, do something.

Pain can be described as the feeling associated with not getting
what we want. The best thing we can do is want something different—
something God wants.

If we decide, instead of avoiding pain, to pursue the lessons and
personal growth that pain is designed to bring to our lives, pain will
do much more than just hurt. It will help you make your life count.

Prayer Time . . . . 5 minutes

*Dear Lord, we know pain will always be a part of our lives, but
we are encouraged that You turned pain into something positive.
Please teach us to allow pain to transform us into believers that
better reflect Your love to the world. In Jesus' name, Amen.*

Next Steps Review . . . . 10 minutes

Icebreaker . . . . 10 minutes

Why do you think some people blame God for their pain and others
embrace God in spite of their pain?

Bible Story: The Crucifixion—*Luke 23:34*

Watch the DVD and fill in the blanks below.

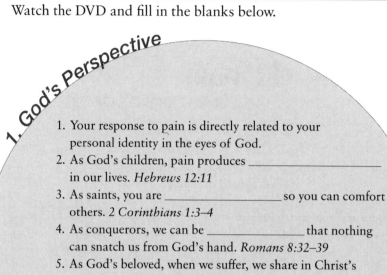

1. God's Perspective

1. Your response to pain is directly related to your personal identity in the eyes of God.
2. As God's children, pain produces _____ in our lives. *Hebrews 12:11*
3. As saints, you are _____ so you can comfort others. *2 Corinthians 1:3–4*
4. As conquerors, we can be _____ that nothing can snatch us from God's hand. *Romans 8:32–39*
5. As God's beloved, when we suffer, we share in Christ's _____. *1 Peter 4:12–14*

3. Intersection

God wants to do something *in* you.

1. Identify and confess the selfishness in your pain response.
2. Ask God to make you more like _____ through your pain.

2. Our Brokenness

Your response to pain will be largely based on your confidence in your "God identity." If we see ourselves as failures, as weak, addictive, and selfish people, we will:

1. View pain only _____.
2. Do almost anything to _____ pain.
3. Seek to drown it out with _____ pleasures.

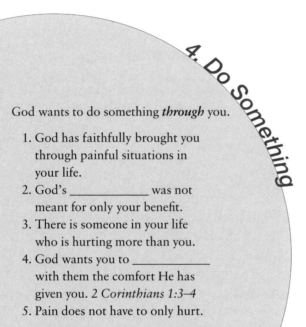

4. Do Something

God wants to do something *through* you.

1. God has faithfully brought you through painful situations in your life.
2. God's _____ was not meant for only your benefit.
3. There is someone in your life who is hurting more than you.
4. God wants you to _____ with them the comfort He has given you. *2 Corinthians 1:3–4*
5. Pain does not have to only hurt.

Read James 4:1–4; 2 Corinthians 1:3–4; Hebrews 12:11.

5. God's Perspective

1. Think about a recent painful time in your life. What did you learn about God's love for you through that experience?

2. (*Optional*) Identify one aspect of the identity God has given you that has been purified through your pain. Be specific in what has changed in how you see yourself and how you act.

3. (*Optional*) If you had to write a manual to Christians on how to deal with pain in a godly way, what would you include?

7. Intersection • Next Steps Preview

Based on what you have learned, describe how you would like to respond in the future to:

Stress

Anger

Unexpected problems

6. Our Brokenness

1. Think about one situation/circumstance when your response to pain *did not* come from your God identity. How did you respond? What did that response produce? What didn't it produce?

2. (*Optional*) Why did you respond that way? How did you view yourself?

3. What did you believe about God that caused you to respond that way?

4. (*Optional*) If you could go back and respond differently, what would you have done?

8. Do Something • Next Steps Preview

Pain doesn't always have to only hurt. Identify one lesson you have learned through your pain and share that with someone who is suffering in a similar way.

As a group, review these Next Step options:

Crawl: Identify one person who is suffering and write a note to them. Include in the note words of encouragement based on comfort you have received from God when you were suffering.

Walk: Make a phone call to someone who is in pain and encourage them.

Run: Visit someone who is suffering and encourage them in person. Pray with them, leave them a gift, and share with them a Bible verse or passage.

Be prepared to report back on what happened.

Group Prayer .... 5 minutes

Dear Lord, thank You for getting us through the painful times in our lives. We also appreciate how You have used them to teach us valuable lessons about who we are. We want to better manage the way we handle our pain and allow it to purify our hearts in a way that helps us be more faithful to the things You want us to do with our lives.

Notes

 **Next Steps**

> *God must do something in me before*
> *He can do something through me.*

Read James 4:1–4.

Describe a common reaction when you don't get your way. For example: when I am stressed, angry, and face unexpected disruptions in my life, I tend to . . .

_____

_____

Based on what you have learned, describe how you would like to respond in the future to:

Stress _____

Anger _____

Unexpected problems _____

Describe God's desired reactions to those incidences. Read Philippians 4:6–8; Matthew 6:19–33; 2 Corinthians 1:3–4.

_____

> *God has a plan to do something through me*
> *for someone, but it might involve pain.*

Crawl

Identify one person who is suffering and write a note to them. Include in the note words of encouragement based on comfort you have received from God when you were suffering.

Dear _____, I am sorry for what you are going through. I do not claim to know exactly what you are going through but recently I experienced a similar trial. (Describe your trial to the degree you feel comfortable.) God taught me a valuable lesson through my experience. (Describe the lesson you learned.) I hope you can benefit from my experience and be confident that God will bring you through your pain and use it to bring power into your life. May God bless you and if I can help you in any way, please let me know.

I will send such a letter to _____ (Name) by _____ (Date).

Walk

Make a phone call to someone who is in pain and encourage him or her.

> Hello _____, I heard what you are going through. I am calling to ask if I can help you in any way.
>
> (Listen for insight on how you can help. If appropriate, share what you learned from your experience.)
>
> I do not claim to know exactly what you are going through but recently I experienced a similar trial. (Describe your trial to the degree you feel comfortable.) God taught me a valuable lesson through my experience. (Describe the lesson you learned.)
>
> I hope you can benefit from my experience and be confident that God will bring you through your pain and use it to bring power into your life.
>
> May God bless you and if I can help you in any way, please let me know.

Run

Visit someone who is suffering and encourage them in person. Pray with them, leave them a gift, and share with them a Bible verse or passage.

Who will you visit? _____

When? _____

Week 4 completed _____ (Date)

Accountability partner's signature: _____

Prayer

Dear Lord, thank You for getting me through the painful times in my life. I also appreciate how You have used them to teach me valuable lessons about who I am. I want to better manage the way I handle my pain and allow it to purify my heart in a way that helps me be more faithful to the things You want me to do with my life.

Preparation for Next Week

Read chapters 21–25: Power.

Make notes on your calendar for those items you have signed up to do at group.

Week 5: Power
The Ability to Do

God gives *you* access to the same power Jesus had.

> Now to Him who is able to do exceedingly abundantly above all that we ask or think, according to the power that works in us, to Him be glory in the church by Christ Jesus to all generations, forever and ever. Amen.
>
> —Ephesians 3:20–21

Power is the authority, ability, and opportunity to *do something*.

God has set aside all the power you will ever need. You cannot *do something* meaningful in the spiritual realm without spiritual power. But before you can acquire spiritual power, you must acknowledge and surrender your human power and strength. The more you surrender, the more you will be empowered.

Prayer Time . . . . 5 minutes

Dear Lord, thank You for providing the spiritual power necessary to do something with our lives. We want to learn to surrender our natural power that we may receive from You the spiritual power to do something like Jesus. In Jesus' name, Amen.

Next Steps Review . . . . 10 minutes

Icebreaker . . . . 10 minutes

Why do we sometimes seem to rely more on our own strength rather than tap into God's power to accomplish His mission?

. . . .

Bible Story: Pilate Threatening Jesus—*John 18:28–19:11*

Watch the DVD and fill in the blanks below.

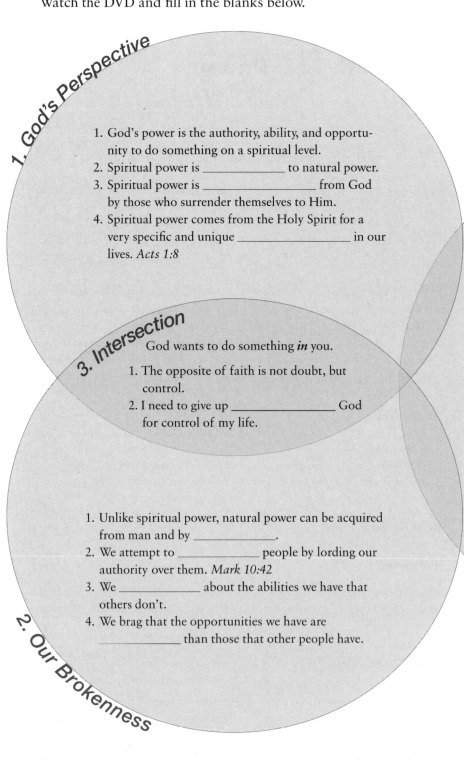

1. God's Perspective

1. God's power is the authority, ability, and opportunity to do something on a spiritual level.
2. Spiritual power is _____ to natural power.
3. Spiritual power is _____ from God by those who surrender themselves to Him.
4. Spiritual power comes from the Holy Spirit for a very specific and unique _____ in our lives. *Acts 1:8*

3. Intersection

God wants to do something *in* you.

1. The opposite of faith is not doubt, but control.
2. I need to give up _____ God for control of my life.

1. Unlike spiritual power, natural power can be acquired from man and by _____.
2. We attempt to _____ people by lording our authority over them. *Mark 10:42*
3. We _____ about the abilities we have that others don't.
4. We brag that the opportunities we have are _____ than those that other people have.

2. Our Brokenness

4. Do Something

God wants to do something *through* you.

1. God wants to reveal to you the _____ nature of the problems that one of your friends has and how He wants to use you to set them free.

2. There is someone in your life who has a problem that can only be solved by God's _____.

3. God plans to help them through someone just like you.

4. Are you willing to be that person?

5. God's Perspective

1. Read Mark 9:25; Luke 8:24; Mark 1:41–42; 5:41–42. What do these verses tell you about Jesus' power?

2. Read 1 Corinthians 12:1–7. What is the purpose of spiritual gifts?

3. Think about the kinds of spiritual opportunities God brings into your life. What seems to come to you most consistently?

4. (*Optional*) What type of service to others brings you the most fulfillment? Praying for someone? Teaching? Evangelism? Encouraging someone? Giving?

5. (*Optional*) Go around the room and tell each other what you see as their God-given strength.

7. Intersection • Next Steps Preview

Discover how God wants to uniquely express His power through you by taking a spiritual gifts test at www.dosomethingworld.org.

- Primary gift _____
- Secondary gift _____

6. Our Brokenness

1. Describe when you last manipulated a situation to get your way using natural power instead of trusting in God.

2. Describe someone you know who has been filled with spiritual power from God. What is different about their handling of a situation from what you have experienced with situations handled through natural power?

3. (*Optional*) Why do you think we are so often driven by power? What is it that we are trying to acquire when we seek power?

8. Do Something • Next Steps Preview

Think of someone with a need that is impossible for your natural power to meet. Pray for God to do something supernatural through you to help them.

As a group, review these Next Step options:

Crawl: After you take the spiritual gifts test during this week's Next Steps, describe in your journal the ideal expression of spiritual power through your life. Identify a specific need someone has for God's powerful hand.

Walk: Identify someone who expresses spiritual power in their life in the way God wants to express the same gift through your life. Spend time with them and take notes on how God expresses His power through them.

Run: Find someone whose need matches the service your spiritual gift is designed to meet and allow God to use you in his or her life.

Bring back a report on what happened.

Group Prayer . . . . .5 minutes

Dear Lord, please provide an opportunity for each of us to help someone in a way that maximizes the intended purpose of Your power in our lives. Give us the courage to step out in faith to allow You to do something powerful through us.

Notes

 **Next Steps**

God must do something in me before
He can do something through me.

Discover how God wants to uniquely express His power through you by taking a spiritual gifts test at www.dosomethingworld.org.

My primary spiritual gift is:

_____

My secondary gift is:

_____

I have noticed that I enjoy doing things that utilize these gifts. (Describe how you enjoy using them—for example: I enjoy teaching because I love organizing the information in a way for people to understand it.)

    1. _____

    _____

    2. _____

    _____

    3. _____

    _____

    4. _____

    _____

Remember, there is someone with a need that is impossible for your natural power to meet. Pray for God to do something supernatural through you to help them.

God has provided the power to
do something through me for someone.

Crawl

- Describe in writing the ideal expression of spiritual power through your life. Identify a specific need someone has for God's powerful hand.

  _____

  _____

- Based on what I know as the ideal expression of my spiritual gift, I would enjoy helping _____ (Name).

- Describe the type of person and need you would enjoy God doing something through you to help.

  _____

  _____

Walk

Identify someone who expresses spiritual power in his or her life in the way God wants to express it through your life. Spend time with them and take notes on how God expresses His power through them.

- _____ is someone who exhibits the gifts I have.

- I will call them by _____ (Date) to set up an appointment to observe their spiritual gift in action.

- By observing my gift in action, I learned that it can be used to . . .

  _____

- I also learned that I will need to rely on other people who can . . .

  _____

- The types of ministries where my gift could be used include . . .

  _____

  _____

Run

Find someone whose need matches the service your spiritual gift is designed to give and allow God to use you in his or her life.

Complete this sentence for your report to the group at your next meeting.

On _____ (Date) God used my gift of _____ to help _____ (encourage, teach, lead them to Christ, feed, clothe, help them get a job, etc.).

As a result God blessed them by (describe what God did in their life)

_____

_____

Week 5 completed _____ (Date)

Accountability partner's signature: _____

Prayer

Dear Lord, please provide an opportunity for me to help someone in a way that maximizes the intended purpose of Your power in my life. Give me the courage to step out in faith to allow You to do something powerful through me.

Preparation for Next Week

Read chapters 26–30: Passion.

Make notes on your calendar for those items you have signed up to do at group.

Week 6: Passion
Never Give Up

You can push through all your obstacles
with the same passion Jesus did.

> But Jesus said to him, "No one, having put his hand to the plow, and looking back, is fit for the kingdom of God."
>
> —Luke 9:62

Without the passion to do something, you will never complete your God-given mission.

Passion will see a light of hope in complete darkness. It is impossible to please God without faith, but there will be times in our life that even the God we put our faith in seems to have forsaken us. It is during those darkest of times that our passion stubbornly keeps believing that God is still there.

Prayer Time . . . . 5 minutes

Dear Lord, thank You for not quitting on us. We know that if we are going to do something with our lives that pleases You, we can never quit. Thank You for preparing us with the passion to finish what You have called us to do. We want to be faithful and completely incorporate everything we learned from this book into our lives. In Jesus' name, Amen.

Next Steps Review . . . . 10 minutes

Icebreaker . . . . 10 minutes

Define *passion*. What are the attributes of a passionate person? What are you most passionate about right now and why?

Bible Story: The End—*John 19:30*

Watch the DVD and fill in the blanks below.

1. God's Perspective

1. By definition, *passion* is your commitment to never give up until you complete what God has called you to do.

2. Living with passion means being fully committed to _____ only on the preparations God has made for you.

3. Living with passion means fulfilling your purpose even if it means loving your enemies while they are in the act of _____ you. *Luke 23:34*

4. Living with passion means _____ walking into painful situations. *Luke 22:41*

5. Passion is so committed to the purpose of God's power that it will drive you to be _____ to it before you are an instrument of His power. *John 18:6; Luke 22:47–51*

6. Passion itself strives each day to hear the Father say, "_____ _____, good and faithful servant." Matthew 25:23

3. Intersection

God wants to do something *in* you.

1. Identify the two top ways you are distracted from _____ what God has called you to do and ask God to cleanse them from your life.

2. Ask God for a description of and desire for completion in everything He asks you to do.

There are three reasons we don't complete the tasks God assigns us:

1. Satan distracts us with _____ benefits to obedience.

2. We don't appreciate the _____ value of the process.

3. We lack the _____ to finish.

2. Our Brokenness

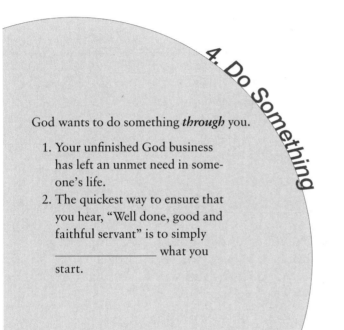

4. Do Something

God wants to do something *through* you.

1. Your unfinished God business has left an unmet need in someone's life.
2. The quickest way to ensure that you hear, "Well done, good and faithful servant" is to simply _____ what you start.

Read Luke 9:62; Proverbs 12:24.

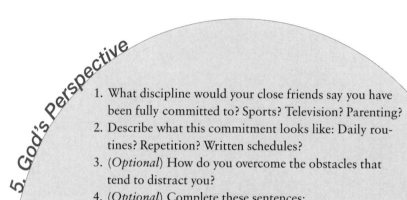

5. God's Perspective

1. What discipline would your close friends say you have been fully committed to? Sports? Television? Parenting?
2. Describe what this commitment looks like: Daily routines? Repetition? Written schedules?
3. (*Optional*) How do you overcome the obstacles that tend to distract you?
4. (*Optional*) Complete these sentences:
   • Overcoming the obstacle makes me feel . . .
   • Being consistent makes me feel . . .

7. Intersection • Next Steps Preview

Identify one spiritual discipline that you want to be consistent in developing. Write out a plan on what consistency looks like and share that with your accountability partner.

6. Our Brokenness

1. Share one spiritual discipline that you have been consistently unable to complete, such as prayer, Bible reading and Bible study, sharing your faith, fasting, or giving.
2. Take a minute to discuss the most common reason you do not complete the task God assigns you. What causes you to quit? Why is it hard to push through to the end?
3. Describe how your relationship with God would improve if you consistently pushed through the obstacles that get in your way.

8. Do Something • Next Steps Preview

As a group, review these Next Step options:

Crawl: Write out one unfinished task from the last six weeks. Go back and complete it.

Walk: Write a six-month plan to do something in line with your spiritual gifts.

Run: By the end of the week, begin executing your six-month plan by having your first meeting with someone you plan to help.

If you are not committed to finish what you start, you might as well not start at all. *Ecclesiastes 5:5*

Great works await you. Don't stop until you experience them.

Remember—God cannot lie. *Hebrews 6:18*

Group Prayer . . . . 5 minutes

Dear Lord, we realize that one day we will die and be held accountable for what we did with our lives. We want You to be pleased with us. We want to hear You say, "Well done, good and faithful servant." We want to commit to You right now that we will do everything through Your power to live every aspect of our lives with passion, in a way that pleases You.

Notes

 **Next Steps**

*God must do something in me before
He can do something through me.*

Identify one spiritual discipline that you want to be consistent in developing. Write out a plan on what consistency looks like and share that with your accountability partner.

God wants me to exercise passion *until
I complete doing something for someone.*

Crawl

Write out one unfinished task from the last six weeks. Go back and complete it.

* In the last six weeks I have not completed . . .

  _____

* I will complete this task by _____ (Date).

Walk

Write a four-step plan to do something in line with your spiritual gifts.

Phase 1—Identify three potential ministries in which you would enjoy serving:

   1. _____
   2. _____
   3. _____

Phase 2—Develop a six-month timeline for learning about them. This can include attending orientation or training classes or simply going to a meeting to observe.

* I will attend a ministry training, orientation class, or go to observe the ministry in action by _____ (Date).

Phase 3—I will begin fulfilling a 90-day commitment to serve in this ministry: _____

Phase 4—Identify one person whom God did something for through you. Help them identify what God wants to do through them. Direct them to take a gifts test, and then identify and get involved in a ministry that matches their gift.

Run

By the end of the week, show your accountability partner your four-week plan from the previous step and begin executing it.

- I will show my plan to _____ by _____ (Date).

- I will attend my first ministry meeting on _____ (Date).

Week 6 completed _____ (Date)

Accountability partner's signature: _____

Prayer

Dear Lord, I realize that one day I will die and be held accountable for what I did with my life. I want You to be pleased with me. I want to hear You say, "Well done, good, faithful, and passionate servant." I want to commit to You right now that I will do everything through Your power to live every aspect of my life in a way that pleases You.

Answer Key

Week 1: The Plan
Step 1
  2. prepared
  3. purpose
  4. pain
  5. power
Step 2
  1. Confidence
  2. Accountability
  3. Nurturing
  4. Trust
Step 3
  1. Acknowledge
  2. Submit
Step 4
  2. through
  3. in need

Week 2: Preparation
Step 1
  2. Holy Spirit
  3. Bible
  4. prayer
  5. faith
  6. opportunities
Step 2
  1. faith
  2. dead
  3. better
Step 3
  2. preparations
Step 4
  1. person
  2. opportunities

Week 3: Purpose
Step 1
  2. obey
  3. truth
Step 2
  1. ignorant
  2. not equipped
  3. reject
Step 3
  1. Seek
  2. Heed
  3. Hide
Step 4
  1. obey
  2. obey

Week 4: Pain
Step 1
  2. righteousness
  3. comforted
  4. confident
  5. glory
Step 2
  1. negatively
  2. avoid
  3. wordly
Step 3
  2. Him
Step 4
  2. comfort
  4. share

Week 5: Power
Step 1
  2. superior
  3. received
  4. purpose
Step 2
  1. force
  2. control
  3. brag
  4. better
Step 3
  2. fighting
Step 4
  1. spiritual
  2. power

Week 6: Passion
Step 1
  2. relying
  3. attacking
  4. voluntarily
  5. subject
  6. Well done
Step 2
  1. counterfeit
  2. purifying
  3. accountability
Step 3
  1. completing
Step 4
  2. finish

Leader's Guide

Guidelines for Leading
a Small Group

What is a small group?

A small group is typically made up of six to twelve people who meet regularly during the week to share about their lives, support one another, and study biblical truths. Each group has a *host* and a *leader* (these may be the same person). Groups can meet in a number of different locations around your city or town—including coffee shops, restaurants, the church and workplaces—but typically they meet in homes. Usually our groups meet in the evening, but you have the freedom to pick a time that is convenient to those in your group.

What is the purpose of a *Do Something!* Small Group?

As a Small Group Leader/Host, your job is to create an environment where people can connect with others, grow through the weekly lessons of the *DO Something!* curriculum, and mature in their relationship with God and others.

Can I get a friend to help me lead?

Absolutely! We encourage you to pair up with another friend or lead as a couple. Together you can pray for the people whom God will bring into your lives. It's our hope that, by teaming up with someone else, it will lighten the load and enhance the experience for both of you.

What if I have to go out of town for a couple of weeks?

Plan ahead. If you have to miss a group and are not co-leading with anyone, simply ask someone in your group to host and facilitate for that meeting. We find that people are willing to take on this responsibility, and just maybe a new leader will be identified to help your group grow. They may even lead a group of their own someday.

Whom should I invite to these meetings in my home?

Invitations and a sample script that you can use when inviting new people to your group are found in appendix B. Perhaps you have formed relationships with people inside your church who haven't found a small group; this is a great opportunity to start! Maybe you have been looking for a way to have a spiritual impact in your workplace. You may even have friends and neighbors who are unwilling to come to church but just might accept an invitation to your home to participate in *DO Something!*

How many people should I expect to be in my group?

We suggest inviting fifteen to thirty people. Then, after the first night, let those in your group invite some of their own friends. In our experience, only about half of those who say they will come actually do come. Don't be discouraged—an optimum number of people to have in a small group is six to twelve, but if more show up, that's fine! If you have less than six people, that's great too. Sometimes the most meaningful connections happen in groups of three to four. Quality of discussion, not quantity of people in the room, is what is most important.

Will I have any responsibilities between the meetings?

Once you form your group, we ask that you connect with your people at least once a week (outside of the meeting time). This can be achieved in a variety of ways: sending an email, making a phone call, or even dropping a postcard in the mail. You may even ask someone in your group to do something to help you take on this responsibility.

Review the lesson for the following week:

- Make sure you read the five chapters of *DO Something! Make Your Life Count* that pertain to the small group lesson.
- Watch the DVD and read the fill-ins and discussion questions in Steps 1–4 in the teaching and discussion sections. (Answer key on p. 78.)
- Contact group members and ask if they need help completing their personal *Do Something* Next Steps.

Will I be asked to continue leading this group after the study is over?

We are very grateful for your gift of leadership for these six (or seven) weeks. When your commitment is over, each leader needs to personally decide what his or her role will be with the group. It's our prayer that the leader/host and group members would continue by making a long-term commitment to continue as a group. If that's not your plan personally, you may be instrumental in helping the group select a new leader and find a place to meet. That's why it's a good idea to share leadership as much as possible during the course of the series.

Is it appropriate to invite non-Christians?

Yes. Our desire, and God's, is to impact men and women for eternity, whoever they are. God has a desire to *do something* in and through everyone. By all means, invite nonbelievers. Serving others just may be the tool God uses in your life to lead someone to salvation.

Who will be there to help me? How can I learn?

No matter if you are a seasoned veteran or a first-time leader, everyone can benefit from having a coach. Even those who are at the pinnacle of their game, like Tiger Woods, depend on a coach to provide positive feedback and support. Coaches are experts at helping others shine. They have a heart for leaders who need encouragement, support, prayer, and a reminder of how important their ministry is to the Kingdom.

How can I get coaching for myself as a leader or host?

Get as much training from your church as possible. Get advice from someone who has hosted or facilitated a group, or even ask them to attend your group and coach you. Learn from small group FAQs online at www.milesmcpherson.com.

How do we handle the "Little People Patrol" or child care needs in our group?

Very carefully! Child care can be a sensitive issue. We suggest you empower the group to openly brainstorm solutions. You may try something that works for some and not for others, so just keep experimenting with ideas. One common solution is to meet in the living room or dining room with the adults and to share the cost of a babysitter (or two) who can be with the kids in a different part of the house. Another popular option is to use one home for the kids and a second home (close by or a phone call away) for the adults. Finally, you could rotate the responsibility of providing a lesson or an activity of some sort for the kids. The last idea can be an incredible blessing to you and the kids. We've done it, and it worked great! Again, the best approach is to encourage the group to dialogue openly about both the problem and the solution.

Can people join after we start?

Yes. Be careful not to close your group and turn it into a clique or a holy huddle. Encourage the group to invite people who are part of the *Do Something* ministry opportunities. If new people come after the study has already begun, encourage people in the group to come alongside the visitors to help them get caught up on the past lessons. Also, do what you can to get them a *DO Something!* book to read.

How do I get people to come to my group?

People must connect to you or people they know before they will connect with your group. Included in appendix B are two scripts you can use to invite people to your small group. Consider these things when inviting people:

Types of people to invite
- family—immediate or extended
- friends
- co-workers
- neighbors
- church contacts

Mistakes to avoid
- failing to saturate the situation in prayer
- giving up too soon
- trying to do all the inviting (encourage those who have committed to your group to invite people also)
- using pressure or manipulation to invite people (don't twist people's arms; instead, ask the Holy Spirit to guide)

- not communicating in a variety of ways (emails, phone calls, postcards)

When should I start inviting?

As soon as you have established a time and place for your meeting. Invite people in a variety of ways. It may be that a random act of kindness will speak to a person louder than words.

Remember, this is a *Do Something* small group. Do as much as you can to get everyone in the group to *Do Something!*

Top 10 Leadership Tips for New Leaders

1. You are a servant leader and not a dominating boss. As a servant leader, your responsibility is to create a safe, positive environment for people to receive new information, build new relationships, and share personal experiences, all of which will help God transform their lives.

2. Be yourself! If you won't be yourself, who will? God wants to use your unique gifts, skills, and temperament. Don't try to do things exactly like another leader; do them the way God has designed you.

If you make a mistake, apologize; if you don't have an answer, apologize and tell them you'll find out later. Your group will love you for it—and you'll sleep better at night.

3. Prepare for your meeting ahead of time. Spend time in prayer asking God to prepare the hearts of everyone who attends. Ask God for the ability to help your group move past the content to the more important issues in life. Be sure to pray for your group members by name. Ask God to use you and your members to touch the heart of every person collectively.

You may even email this prayer list (minus any confidential or sensitive information) to your members so everyone can get in on what God is doing in your midst.

4. Occasionally break up into smaller groups. This can be very powerful, especially after the group gets comfortable with one another. Sub-grouping involves breaking up into prayer partners or triads after the session. It's easier for people to apply what they are learning if they experience a little love and support. Also, those who are unaccustomed to praying out loud will feel more comfortable trying it with just one or two others.

Remind these smaller groups that they don't have to pray out loud if they feel uncomfortable!

5. Ask as many clarifying questions as possible before you give answers. This will help clarify their question and give others an opportunity to get involved. Seek first to understand, then to be understood. The old adage is true: "People don't care how much you know, until they know how much you care."

It's very important that you respond well to those who take the risk of answering your questions. Remember to affirm a person when they speak even if they give the wrong answer. If you disagree, take the blame for the miscommunication and then restate the question for clarity. Then ask, "How about someone else?" Keep in mind that it will be very intimidating for some people to either ask or answer a question, or to give input. Since there will be penetrating questions each week, you will need to be sensitive to this through the entire study.

Use the 30–70 rule: Good leaders speak 30 percent of the time and allow the group to speak 70 percent of the time.

6. When you ask a question, be patient. Someone will eventually respond. Sometimes people need a moment to think about the question, and if silence doesn't bother you, it won't bother anyone else.

7. Show interest with your body language. One of the best ways to connect with people is to actively listen to them. Great listeners not only use their ears but their entire body. When thinking about listening nonverbally, remember the acronym SOLER, which stands for:

face people **S**quarely
adopt an **O**pen posture
Lean slightly forward
maintain good **E**ye contact
be **R**elaxed and natural

85

8. Listen for the "crickets." Be ready for those awkward moments of silence, when all you can hear are the crickets. It's incredibly important for facilitators to be sensitive to new people or others in their group who are a little reluctant or are not ready to add to the conversation or to pray out loud. If you notice the "crickets," try not to put added pressure on people who are not ready to share by going "around the circle" for prayer requests or comments. Instead, encourage individuals gently by asking questions like: "How about someone else?" or "Would someone who hasn't shared like to add anything?"

9. How to control the motor mouth. Handling a group member who intentionally or unintentionally dominates your group time can be one of the biggest challenges for facilitators. It's important at the outset of the group to share that it's your hope that everyone in the group gets a chance to add to the group discussion. If a group member doesn't "take the hint" from your suggestion of asking people who haven't yet shared to share, then it's probably appropriate to take more drastic steps. One easy way to dissuade the constant talker is to make sure you limit your eye contact with this person. When you make eye contact, it communicates to the dominator that it's appropriate to speak. You may want to strategically sit this person next to you. If the behavior persists, it may be appropriate to pull the person aside after the meeting and ask them to help you encourage others to share by praying privately for those individuals who are reluctant to join in.

10. Rely on God. This is not about you, and the transformation in the people will be done by God. Pray before, during, and after a meeting. Then God will have His way with you and your group. *See Zechariah 4:6.*

Preparing for the First Meeting

Small Group Starter Kit Checklist

- Participant's Guide
- *DO Something!* DVD
- *DO Something! Make Your Life Count* book
- Forms from appendix C:
    - Small Group Contact List
    - Little People Patrol (child care)
    - Munchies Sign-up Sheet
- Extra Bibles and pens
- Refreshments or potluck assignments*

Creating the Right Mood the First Night

The Bible is very clear on the subject of offering hospitality. First Peter 4:9 states, "Open your homes to each other without complaining." Or simply put, open hearts lead to open homes. For some, hospitality is as natural as breathing; for others, the practice must be acquired. Unfortunately, many Christians have confused biblical hospitality with entertaining. Entertaining says: "I want to impress you with my beautiful home, my clever decorating, and my gourmet

*The six-week study works best with simple refreshments, for the sake of time; the seven-week study allows time for a potluck.

87

cooking." Conversely, hospitality seeks to minister. It says, "This home is not mine. It's truly a gift from my Master. I am His servant and I use it as He desires." Hospitality puts away pride and doesn't care if people see real humanness. And because there are no false pretensions, people can relax and are more open to friendship. With that said, there's nothing wrong with a beautiful home, clever decorating, and good food.

- Before the meeting, dedicate your home and its contents to the Lord. Is there anything that you would be embarrassed for Jesus to see if He was coming for dinner?
- Prepare for the meeting ahead of time; make sure there are plenty of seats, organized in as close to a circle as possible.
- If possible, put the pets away so they won't be a distraction during meeting time.
- Turn on lights inside the rooms that you want your guests to have access to. Shut doors and turn off lights in places that are off limits.
- If parking is tight, it's a good idea to let your neighbors know that you'll be having a get-together once a week. Make sure your guests know where they're allowed to park.
- Make sure everyone has a name tag, and spend a little time with each guest to get to know them. Don't want to use name tags? Instead, play a "name game" using alliteration or rhyming to make up funny names—for example, the first person says, "I'm "Candy Andy." The person to their right goes next by introducing themselves, "Hi, I'm Marky Mark. And that's Candy Andy." The next person goes, "Hi, I'm Pip-squeak Paul. That's Marky Mark and he's Candy Andy." The game continues around the entire circle, so everyone gets a turn to introduce themselves and a shot at remembering the group members' names. It will be corny, but it will be fun.

Week 1: Options for a Seven-Week Study

The first week has extra material that will make it a longer meeting than the other five sessions. It includes an orientation and a snack or meal break. The option is available to divide this into two weeks if you prefer to keep all meetings to approximately 90 minutes. If you choose to go this route, notify group members that the series will add an introductory Zero Week to kick off the six-week study. (See the Leader's Notes for the First Week.)

Session Format

From the Week 1 Overview through Week 6, each meeting has seven parts. It will be important to balance the time goal allocated for each part of the agenda, but do not race through so fast you sacrifice meaningful ministry. Familiarize yourself with the format by reviewing pages 14–16.

Meeting Overview

1. Settle In
2. Prayer Time
3. Review of *Do Something* Next Steps from previous week
4. Icebreaker
5. Part 1: DVD Teaching—complete fill-ins for Steps 1–4 in circle diagrams
6. Part 2: Group Discussion of Steps 5–8 in circle diagrams
7. Prayer Time

Leadership Guidelines

1. Settle In.. 5 minutes
   a. Make sure that
      • the kids are in their room;
      • everyone has a good seat and is comfortable; and
      • everyone has a pen, their curriculum, and their Bible.

b. Read the opening statement, Scripture verse, and paragraph(s).

2. **Prayer Time**. . . . . 10 minutes
   a. Ask for prayer requests from the group.
   b. Have one person open the meeting with prayer or invite people to pray for someone in the room. (Don't force anyone to pray.) An opening prayer is provided at the beginning of the Overview of Week 1 and at the beginning of Weeks 2–6.
   c. Prayer time has two parts:
      i. Praying for specific requests.
      ii. Praying for the lesson topic itself. (Two pre-written prayers for each week are provided for people to read. They will help focus the prayers on the intended lesson and also empower people who are nervous about praying in public to *do something* about it).

3. *Do Something* **Next Steps Review**
   (from the previous week) . . . . 10 minutes
   Review the results of the Step 7 Intersection and/or Step 8 from the previous week. Every week there will be a *Do Something* challenge—one to be completed on ourselves and one on behalf of someone else. During the *Do Something* recap time, you can give two or three people an opportunity to share either what God did *to* them, in their own hearts, or what God did *through* them in the life of someone else. Be careful that this time isn't more than ten minutes. Encourage each member to share their full stories with other members of the group outside the small group meeting. This will foster stronger relationships and give them an opportunity to encourage one another.

4. **Icebreaker**. . . . . 10 minutes
   This is a leading question designed to get the group thinking about and focused on the session's topic.

91

5. Part 1: DVD Teaching . . . . 10 minutes
Ask everyone to turn to his or her lesson in Part 1: Teaching—
and refer to the circles. (See pages 14–15 in the Orientation for
a more detailed discussion of Steps 1–4.)

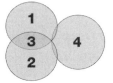

Start the DVD and fill in the blanks in Steps 1–4.
NOTE: The answer key is on page 78.

6. Part 2: Group Discussion . . . . 45 minutes
Once the DVD is done, turn the page and conduct the discus-
sion in the same circles format for Steps 5 and 6.

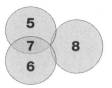

Some questions are marked "Optional"—if you have limited
time, you may need to exclude these.

Steps 7 and 8 preview the Next Steps for the week. (See
pages 15–16 for a more detailed discussion of Steps 5–8 and
Do Something Next Steps.)

7. Prayer Time . . . . 10 minutes
After everyone is clear on their *Do Something* Next Steps,
close with a word of encouragement to complete their Next
Steps and weekly reading assignment, and then pray. A group
prayer is available at the end of each week's session.

Leader's Notes for the First Week

Because Week 1, with its orientation, is a unique session of the study, these leader's notes are provided to help you facilitate the first meeting. As mentioned earlier, Week 1 is laid out so it can be divided into two weeks if desired.

For a seven-week series, the first week becomes Zero Week, which ends after the Orientation. Look for *Zero Week* options along the way.

For a six-week series, continue on through the Overview after a short break.

Preview

- Before the meeting begins, if you plan to have someone else close the meeting in prayer, discuss it with them so they are prepared to do so. (Make this a weekly practice to avoid potential embarrassment to a group member.) A group prayer is written out for this purpose at the end of each week's study.
- After the initial introductory material, you will cover the format of the weekly sessions, reviewing a typical meeting with your small group. Going through the format of the meeting and what will be expected each week will help ease the nervousness of the unknown. It is about God doing something in and through us.
- You will discuss the three basic parts of each session—Teaching, Discussion, and *Do Something* Next Steps—so that members

understand the eight steps within the four-part paradigm of each meeting.

- As mentioned earlier, an answer key for the Teaching sections is located on page 78.
- Familiarize yourself with the material in the four appendixes.

The following pages mirror the study guide text from Week 1, interspersed with shaded leader's notes to facilitate your leadership of the meeting. Notes specific to Zero Week are labeled accordingly. When you reach the Break, use the column with the option you have chosen.

....

Week 1: The Plan
Orientation and Overview

The goal of Week 1 is for members of the group to get acquainted, to talk about the basics of the session format, and to move into the *DO Something!* experience.

For groups who choose to divide Week 1 into two weeks, the first week—Zero Week—includes the Orientation and ends with a potluck or meal (pp. 13–16), and Week 1 picks up with the Overview of the 5 P's (pp. 17–26).

 ***Orientation***   *Zero Week*

Getting to Know Your Group . . . . 10 minutes

> Here are two options for getting to know each other (whether or not you choose to use name tags). If you use the second option, you can combine the "Share" question with their individual introductions.
>
> - If you have a lively group, try a "name game" like the one described on page 88.

> • If you want to keep things more low key, ask the participants to briefly give their name and some information about what they do, their family, or their job—whatever information they feel comfortable sharing.

- Take a few minutes to get to know each other.
- Share: What is the number one reason you have chosen to be a part of this Do Something journey?

Introduction to the *DO Something!* Experience .... 10 minutes

- Watch the welcome message from Miles McPherson.
- Review the letter from Miles on page 5.
- Review the MyTown, USA, map on page 206 in the book.

> Ask the group members to briefly discuss what each of them knows about their own church and community as compared to the My Town map. (Leave the rest of the Challenge material for the following segment.)

What Is the Ultimate Goal of the Group? .... 5 minutes

> **NOTE:** *It is critical to let people know that, even though this is about doing something, no one will be forced to do something by the people in the group. Reinforce this at the end of the meeting.*

1. Become a Do Something believer who is actively engaged in doing something obedient to God as an individual.
2. Accept the *DO Something!* Challenge on pages 205–8 in the book and become part of the solution to one of your community's problems. Join or start a ministry designed to bring Christ's love to your broken world.

> ***ZERO WEEK***—Review the *DO Something!* Challenge on pages 205–8, ask the group members to skim through the list of twenty-five ministries, and allow a few minutes for comments.

Format of Weekly Sessions................................... 10 minutes

After a review of the previous week's material, the core of the meeting covers eight steps, represented by circles in your guide. Following is a description of each step.

Teaching

Participants will watch a DVD teaching from Miles McPherson while completing these four steps:

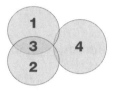

Step 1—God's Perspective

In Step 1 you will learn God's perspective on your life. God's perspective of your life is based on His unconditional love for you and His plans to use you to do great things in the world. The DVD teaching will guide everyone through the fill-in-the-blank questions about the lesson's topic. *An answer key is on page 78.*

Step 2—Our Brokenness

You will then skip down to Step 2 and look at your brokenness. Because of our brokenness, we have a very distorted view of our lives. We simply do not see ourselves like God does, and it's important for us to understand the extent to which our brokenness influences our decisions. The DVD teaching will guide everyone through the fill-in-the-blank questions about how our brokenness affects our perspective.

Step 3—Intersection

Step 3 lies in between the circles for Steps 1 and 2. Ministry happens when our brokenness intersects with and is submitted to God's ideal perspective for our lives. It is then that we must make a decision to do something to submit ourselves to His plan for our lives. The DVD teaching will guide everyone through the fill-in-the-blank questions about the lesson's topic.

Step 4—Do Something

Once you experience what God wants to do *in* you, you are ready for Him to do something *through* you. In Step 4 you will learn about applying your internal "do something" to help someone else in his or her time of need. Ministry happens when you apply the changes that God has made in your life to help someone else.

Discussion

After viewing the DVD teaching, a group discussion follows the same four steps. This is your opportunity to internalize the lesson and discuss how it applies to you.

Step 5—God's Perspective

Discuss what you've learned about God's perspective on your life.

Step 6—Our Brokenness

Discuss how your brokenness can distract you from God's perspective on His plan in your life.

Step 7—Intersection • Next Steps Preview

Now that you have learned two opposing views—God's perspective and how you view life through your brokenness—it is time to discuss what you need to allow God to do in your life to bring about His desired change. Keep in mind: what God does *in you* is going to lead to His doing something *through you*. This step will help prepare you for Step 8 and the practical *Do Something* Next Steps that you will complete during the week.

Step 8—Do Something • Next Steps Preview

The last discussion will prepare you to practically apply what you have learned and experienced to help someone who is in need.

You will have three *Do Something* Next Steps options. Each step builds on the previous one, starting with something simple in the first step. *Do only what you feel comfortable doing.*

Crawl—This will usually be something simple you can do alone and most often contains a form of planning.

Walk—This step is a little more aggressive *do something* and usually involves contacting someone via email, phone, or letter.

Run—This step will usually involve making personal contact with someone.

Each week you will be encouraged to bring back a report on what you did.

You'll also be asked to find an accountability partner to help you stay on track as you work through this study.

NOTE: "*(Optional)*" is placed next to questions you can respond to as time allows.

Do Something Next Steps

The *Do Something* Next Steps are what you are responsible to do on your own outside the group meeting. These pages are designed to guide you through what you have been challenged to do in Step 8 of the week's lesson. You can also use these pages as a journal to record what happens.

Small Group "I Do's"

Review the Small Group Guidelines in appendix A (pp. 101–2).

> Have the members read through the Seven Small Group "I Do's." You may want to ask someone to read these aloud as the group follows along. Ask if anyone has any questions.
>
> Then have the group discuss the points in the agreement on page 102. Fill in the blanks and date the agreement.
>
> *ZERO WEEK*—Circulate the sign-up sheets from appendix C, encouraging group members to choose a date for Munchies and Little People Patrol as decided earlier.

Choose the appropriate week to follow on the next page.

ZERO WEEK   **WEEK 1**

Prayer

Finish your first meeting as the leader with a word of prayer for God's blessing on the *DO Something!* experience. If you're nervous, uncomfortable, or want to give someone else a chance to pray, here is a prayer you can use:

Dear Lord, thank You for everyone who is here tonight. Lord, we believe that You want to do something with our lives that is bigger than us. We believe in the promise You made in John 14:12, that if we trusted You, You would empower us to do something even greater than You did. We do not know how that would happen, but we are here to find out. Please bless the next six weeks we will spend together. May they lay a foundation in our hearts to live a Do Something life. In Jesus' name, Amen.

Break

Time for the potluck!

Next week's session starts with "An Overview of the 5 P's" on page 17. Follow the format in the participant's section through Step 8.

Break

Use this snack or meal time to complete the sign-up sheets for contact information, refreshments, and child care as your group leader requests.

Take a minute to recue the DVD so you're ready to play the first lesson: The Plan. Call the group back together about 10 minutes into the break.

99

Turn to page 17 and begin the first *DO Something!* lesson, An Overview of the 5 P's. After covering the introductory material to that section—the 5 P's, the Scripture, and the introductory paragraph—and positioning the participants to see the TV, begin the DVD.

Return to Wrapping Up (below) after the group finishes Step 8 of the Discussion on page 21 to close the meeting.

Wrapping Up Week 1: The Plan

To wrap up the meeting,

* make sure everyone understands their *Do Something* weekly application in Step 8 and in Next Steps;

* remind them that they will be finding an accountability partner this week;

* encourage the group to read the assigned section of the book;

* ask members to finish filling out the roster and sign-up sheets;

* dismiss with a word of prayer, using the Group Prayer at the end of Step 8 if desired.

Group Prayer . . . . 5 minutes

Dear Lord, we know that You have a plan to put us in a position to do something great through our lives. We ask that You reveal Your plan to us each day. Please give us the faith to allow You to lead us through that plan.

Appendix A

Small Group Guidelines

Seven Small Group "I Do's"

I DO know that I cannot reach spiritual maturity alone.

I DO believe that God can use this small group as a source of spiritual accountability in my life.

I DO agree to be faithful to the group by doing my best to attend every meeting, calling ahead when I cannot make it, and actively participating each week.

I DO commit to doing what I can to make this a safe place for others to experience God by not gossiping, by not being negative, and by respecting confidentiality.

I DO commit to submitting myself to the Holy Spirit, allowing Him to mold me into a new person.

I DO promise to invite new people to the group.

I DO pray that everyone in this group will DO Something for God that they never thought possible in their life.

We agree to the following:

- Meals or snacks _____

- Child care _____

- When we will meet (day of the week)

  _____

- Where we will meet (place)

  _____

- We will begin at (time) _____ and end at _____

Date of this agreement _____/_____/_____

Appendix B

Invitation Scripts

1. Important points to cover when calling those from your church who have requested to become part of a group:

- Introduce yourself by name, mention the church you attend, and ask if they have a moment to talk.
- Indicate that you are starting a new group and would like to invite them to participate in a six-week [seven-week] study in your home on _____ at _____ (day of the week and time that you have selected).
- Explain that the focus will be to study how we can *Do Something* to make a difference in our community, based on the life of Jesus. Explain to them there will be a ten-to-fifteen-minute video teaching each week followed by a group discussion time.
- If they plan to attend, provide your phone number, home address, email address, and directions to your home. Reconfirm the date and the time.
- Be sure to get their email address before you end the call.
- End with an inviting closing such as: "I can't wait to have you in my home" or "I'm looking forward to you joining us."
- Follow up with a reminder card or email four to five days before the time of the meeting.

- You can also have someone design an Evite to send out to friends and family.

2. **Important points to cover when inviting a neighbor to your group:**

- Introduce yourself by name as their neighbor. Ask if they have a moment to talk.
- Indicate that you are planning to have a group of neighbors meet in your home on _____ at _____ (day of the week and time) for a six-week [seven-week] Bible study.
- Explain that the focus will be to study how we can *Do Something* to make a difference in our community, based on the life of Jesus. Explain to them there will be a ten-to-fifteen-minute video teaching each week followed by a group discussion time.
- If yes: Provide your phone number, address, and email address with directions, and reconfirm the date and time.
- Follow up with a reminder card or email four to five days before the time of the meeting.
- End with an inviting closing such as, "I can't wait to have you in my home," or "I'm looking forward to you joining us," or "Please feel free to come if you change your mind."
- If no: Thank them and offer your telephone number just in case they change their mind.

Appendix C

Sign-Up Sheets

Small Group Contact List

Name	Phone #	Email

Little People Patrol (Child Care)

Name & Phone #

Week 1_____

Week 2_____

Week 3_____

Week 4_____

Week 5_____

Week 6_____

Munchies Sign-Up

Name & Phone #

Week 1_____

Week 2_____

Week 3_____

Week 4_____

Week 5_____

Week 6_____

Appendix D

AWCIPA

Sample Prayers

In order to keep your prayers focused, spend a given amount of time on each letter, one at a time. Avoid jumping around. Add your own verses to each category. Praying God's Word is our way to hold Him to His own promises. Remember, it is impossible for God to lie (Heb. 6:18).

A—Admire and thank God.

Read Psalm 8:9 and then thank God for everything you can think of.

> Thank You, God, for Your awesome power and love. You are amazing in all that You do and provide. Your name is so majestic all through the earth. Thank You, God.
>
> Steve J.

Psalm 57:9–10; Psalm 150; Psalm 9:1

W—Wait quietly before God.

Read Psalm 46:10 and then sit quietly and listen to God speak to you and write it down.

Thank You, God, for being my strength, for when I am still, You shield me from the fire. Thank You for protecting me from the enemy.

Samuel M.

Other verses that encourage you to wait: Psalm 27:14; 1 Kings 19:11–13; Psalm 59:9

C—Confess your sin.

Read 1 John 1:9 and then confess your sins to God.

Dear Lord, I know that I have sinned. Please forgive me of all the wrong I've done and help me and keep me pure. If I confess my sins, You are faithful and just and will forgive me of my sins and purify me of all unrighteousness. Lord, I love You and I thank You for all of my family and my life.

Mallorie G.

Psalm 139:23–24; James 5:16; Psalm 103:11–12

I—Intercede for others.

Read Philippians 1:3–6 and then pray for other people.

Lord, I want to serve You faithfully with my whole heart. May I not sin against You by failing to pray for others. I pray for the needs of my brothers and sisters in Christ. May their hearts be turned toward You. May they do what is good and right.

Phyllis M.

Matthew 5:44; James 5:14–15; 1 Samuel 12:23–25

P—Petition for yourself.

Read Psalm 51:10–12 and then ask for a pure heart; ask for a physical, financial, or emotional need to be met.

God, please make my heart pure and let my eyes be set on You. Help me to stay pure and continue to stay steadfast in my walk with You.

Peter Z.

Psalm 19:12–14; John 14:13–14; 1 Chronicles 4:10

A—Admire and thank God.

Once again, read Psalm 8:9 and then thank God for everything you can think of.

> I praise You, Lord! Your name is majestic above all names. You alone are worthy of our prayer and worship. I praise You, Lord! You alone are the one worthy of my praise.
>
> Monique W.

Psalm 57:9–10; Psalm 150; Psalm 9:1

Miles McPherson is the senior pastor of the Rock Church in San Diego. A former defensive back with the San Diego Chargers, he is president and founder of Miles Ahead Ministries, an evangelistic ministry focused on sharing the good news of Jesus Christ with teens and adults all over the world. Miles and his wife, Debbie, have three children and live in San Diego.

Visit Miles's website at
www.milesmcpherson.com.

Through the Miles Ahead ministries evangelistic events, over 45,000 people have given their lives to the Lord in events in thirteen cities since 1996. A Miles Ahead Festival consists of the Do Something leadership conference, community service projects, and evening evangelistic events.

For information on hosting a
Miles Ahead Youth Evangelistic Festival,
go to www.milesahead.tv.